THE ART
of the
AESTHETIC
PRACTICE

7 Fundamental Steps to Providing
the Ultimate Patient Experience
and Maximizing Profitability

ASHLEY CLOUD

The Art of the Aesthetic Practice

7 FUNDAMENTAL STEPS TO PROVIDING THE ULTIMATE PATIENT EXPERIENCE AND MAXIMIZING PROFITABILITY

By
ASHLEY CLOUD

Table of Contents

Introduction

"Inside every block of marble lies a beautiful statue."
~ Michelangelo

It's hard to believe it was almost two decades ago that I joined a plastic surgery practice as a Patient Coordinator, beginning an amazing journey in the medical aesthetics realm. I knew nothing about plastic surgery but managed to land the job anyhow. At that time everything was paper scheduling books, paper charts, and typewriters. We did not have access to the vast amount of data for measuring and benchmarking available to practices today. We basically followed the "be nice and patients will buy from you sales model," and patients essentially bought because they did think we were nice and trusted in my surgeons to do a great job.

Fast forward to today, the times have certainly changed. We are no longer in an "I only have to be nice to sell" environment. Today's patient, particularly the aesthetic patient, actually demonstrates more consumer behaviors than patient behaviors. You've probably heard the phrase "consumers vote with their feet," meaning if they are not provided with a top-notch experience they will go elsewhere. Even "satisfied" patients will go elsewhere if there's a better deal down the road by a competitor.

The key is to build a tribe of loyal patients who will not only stay with your practice through thick & thin, but who will also be "walking patient billboards" out in the community advocating for your practice.

I wrote this book to help practices identify the aesthetic patient's buying habits, and to use this knowledge to best position the practice to exceed patient needs. In this book I will show you proven strategies to attract & retain emotionally invested clients who become your biggest advocates.

As the title suggests, this book meant to relay fundamental steps, or basic principles, to providing patients with the ultimate experience with your practice. The recommendations in this book are a culmination of years of observations & data collection, teachings of mentors & colleagues, and practical application.

You will find fresh and new ideas to help your practice maintain a competitive advantage. You will also find tried and true strategies that have been around for years simply because they have stood the test of time.

Adversely, this book is NOT meant to be a comprehensive analysis of the "inner workings" of a practice, nor is it meant to be a deep dive into all of the processes a practice must adopt in order to achieve profitable success.

Disclaimer: I am not a medical doctor or clinical provider, and nothing in this book should be construed as medical advice!

After years of working with practices, I can tell you with certainty you will get very little result if you do not implement what you learn. I have worked with hundreds of practices and staff members to help them succeed and meet their goals. This book will provide you with action steps you can use daily to provide an ultimate experience for your patients that drives retention & referrals, thus increasing your bottom line.

Although you will see results faster if you put ALL of the steps listed in this book into practice, even implementing just a few will be beneficial. I recommend starting with one new action a week if it helps make the adaptation more manageable. The goal here is consistency.

Note: I've intentionally made this a quick read, so even the busiest of people can get through it at lightning speed. The price is also intentionally low so even people with the smallest of budgets can afford it.

I am excited to take this journey with you, and I always welcome any questions or comments. Feel free to reach out any time: info@ashley-cloud.com.

Cheers to success, empowerment, patient engagement, and profitability!

Ashley

About The Author

Ashley Cloud is a consultant, speaker, trainer, and author. Having spent over 19 years in the medical aesthetics industry in both administrative and consulting roles, Ashley understands the importance of empowering physicians & their staff with tools they can use to provide the ultimate patient experience for their patients, while dramatically increasing retention, referrals, and, of course, their bottom line. Ashley identifies & addresses areas of growth opportunity in all aspects of a business, to include people, processes, and procedures, and provides strategic action plans to help practices reach their goals quickly.

Ashley lives in Colorado with her husband, dogs & horses ~ aka "the kids."

Step 1: Overcoming Common Myths

"The great enemy of the truth is very often not the lie, deliberate, contrived and dishonest, but the myth, persistent, persuasive and unrealistic." ~ John F. Kennedy

The first step toward creating the ultimate patient experience is actually not a patient facing step at all but is instead a change in mindset. Whenever I begin a consulting partnership with a practice or medical spa, I frequently hear one or more of the following objections:

1. Our patients are different.
2. Our practice / doctor is different.
3. I / we are not in sales.

First, let me say I understand the thought processes fueling these 3 common myths – I used to believe them myself! However, after years of research and data-based consulting, I realized I had to overcome those beliefs and change my mindset about the patient buying habits and my role in the sales process. The proof is in the data gathered from hundreds of practices over the years.

Believing one or all of these myths can be a "crutch" at best, and extremely debilitating to a practice at worst.

The following statements are based on the law of averages. Of course, there will always be 'outliers' but for all intent and purposes of this book, statements made will be based on the majority average. It is this segment that provides practice growth and requires most attention. Now, let's dissect each of these myths further.

Our patients are different: Okay, I agree wholeheartedly there will be basic characteristic differences in patients. There are socio-economic differences, gender differences, educational differences, age differences. We are a great big world of different people and this is a good thing!

That said, statistics clearly show that all consumers, regardless of these fundamental differences, have the same basic buying habits. It's widely believed consumers make purchasing decisions based on emotion and then rationalize the purchase with logic. It is up to us in the practice to tap into that emotional need while providing the logic the consumer patient requires to make a purchase.

In fact, the aesthetic patient actually demonstrates more *consumer* behaviors than patient behaviors in their buying processes (at least up to the time of the procedure and subsequent recovery). This means we must understand consumer behaviors in order to fully understand the aesthetic patient's needs. Yes, THEY ARE SHOPPING!

When you learn to communicate and relate with the patient at the consumer level, you will see the average patient has a defined set of key purchasing drivers that is not influenced by fundamental differences listed above.

Our practice is different: As with the patient myth, every individual practice will have wonderful identifying qualities that make them unique in the aesthetic industry. Again, this is a great thing as it sets you apart!

That said, I quite often hear practices say they are different from other practices in that they are not "salesy." In their attempt to not be a salesperson, they may encourage patients to "go home and think about the consultation recommendations" before buying, sometimes even if the patient is ready to buy while in the office.

Or, they may not provide a call to action such as asking the patient if they are ready to schedule the procedure because they do not want to be "pushy like other practices."

When conducting onsite practice evaluations, I've seen patients leave the office with no quote estimate, instead being told it would be emailed to them in the following day.

It is my experience this is often done to avoid the face-to-face "money conversation." The trouble is, these are all lost opportunities to help the patient move to the next stage of their relationship with the practice.

We will address sales (and how to sell without being a "pushy salesperson") in Step 5. For now, let's agree the patient has a perceived need and they have obviously come to you for your expertise & help. If you have the best solution for the patient and can truly help them, it is your moral obligation to do so.

Here's a fun (and statistically proven) fact: the more people that schedule a procedure on the day of their consultation (i.e. the same day scheduling rate), the higher your overall patient conversion rate will be. There is a direct correlation between same day scheduling rates and overall scheduling rates.

Higher patient conversion rates generally equal higher profitability. So, do you see how by believing in this myth, many practices actually sabotage the very revenue growth they hope to achieve?

I / we are not in sales: Unless you are extremely wealthy and can afford to give away your services for free, I am assuming you need revenue coming in to pay salaries, purchase equipment, keep the lights on, and procure other miscellaneous items. To maximize profitability you must adopt, or fine-tune, strategic processes that increase patient attraction, retention, and advocacy. At the very core of these processes you will find sales fundamentals.

Data consistently shows practices that have sales processes in place move the aesthetic patient more easily through every stage in their journey, making the process not only less stressful for the patient, but for the practice as well.

Again, we will discuss sales in depth in Step 5, but for now I only ask that you consider the notion that sales processes must be adopted in order to meet and exceed the practice's financial goals. This puts every member of the team in a sales role in some capacity if they hope to contribute to the practice's success.

Step 2: Build A Winning Team

"You cannot build an empire on sand." ~ author unknown

Your staff is your practice's #1 most valuable asset. The employees you hire can make or break your business, literally. They provide the foundation from which all other business structures are built and represent the "face of the practice" on every level.

I recently watched a Stanford Graduate School of Business interview in which financial mogul and Blackstone Chairman CEO Stephen Schwarzman stresses the importance of hiring someone who can "articulate the core values of your business." Your staff should be a reflection of your practice's core values.

But how do you ensure your staff is a reflection of your core values? First and foremost, they need to understand what the practice's core values really are. Do you have a mission statement? Does it reside in a prominent area where it can be seen by staff and patients alike?

A mission statement is your promise to your patients, employees, and business that reflects your goals and values. It is your "big why," the reason your practice exists.

A mission statement consists of the following: "Who" the statement is for, "What" it is you do, and "Why" you do it. My mission statement is as follows:

"Empowering aesthetic medical practices, providers, and spas to create world-class services by implementing strategic, patient-centric, and results driven processes that generate a meaningful profit and transform patient's lives."

It is also important to make sure your staff understands the practice's goals. I oftentimes ask staff members about practice goals and the answer is usually something along the lines of, "To make more money?"

Making more money is a universal wish, but a goal is more defined. A goal should be very specific, strategic, and measurable. An example would be "To be a 100% cash-based business in 12 months" or "To have a procedure mix of 75% breast augmentations and 25% other body procedures."

Knowledge of specific practice goals help the staff focus on the steps required to reach the desired outcome. "Make more money" leaves too much open for interpretation. What specific steps will you take to make more money? A clear goal helps drive actions that will positively affect the outcome of the goal.

Let's use the breast augmentation goal mentioned above. One good strategy would be Schedule Templating. In this case, your staff would strategically block the consultation schedule so there are ample and designated slots open for breast augmentation patients. The number of breast augmentation slots needed per clinic day depends on your end goal (i.e. your target # of breast augmentation procedures you hope to complete in a given time period), your average breast augmentation consult – surgery conversion rate, and the realistic number of appointment slots available during the given time period.

The point is to ensure you are leaving the schedule open for your targeted breast augmentation patients, and to selectively make sure you are not spending prime appointment real estate consulting with procedures you do not wish to be performing, and that would not help you reach your breast augmentation goal.

Next, it is crucial to make the right hiring decisions. I often see practices make a quick hiring decision based solely on the applicant having experience in another practice and/or being in possession of general office skills. They do this without considering the specialized skills required for the employee to be successful in the aesthetic environment: sales and relationship building skills.

Other highly desirable skills include "coachability" and a desire to learn and be part of a team. Basic skills can be taught (to include procedural knowledge) but a desire to participate in successful outcomes can be hard to transfer. I cannot agree more with the quote "Hire for Attitude, Train for Skill."

Employees that are willing to go above and beyond their daily requirements, and that are committed to the concept of practice growth, are invaluable. Help them stay at the top of their game by investing in their development. This could be via webinars, external or internal classes, association meetings, or books. Continuing education for staff development is paramount for employee retention, practice success, and competitive advantage.

There is a direct correlation between employee satisfaction and patient satisfaction. Happy staff tend to drive happy patients. Goodwill and trust flow in a happy practice. It is infectious. It creates a happy culture that is noticed and embraced by your patients.

The opposite of this is also true. I have been in practices where you could cut the tension with a knife. It is an interesting phenomenon; I can almost always guess the demeanor of the physician before even meeting him or her simply by observing the collective demeanor of his or her staff. Providers who are curt or not open to change will usually have staff that are curt and not open to change.

Employees who feel valued and are happy at work are 12% more productive than those who do not (source: Adecco). There are a number of ways to create or maintain employee satisfaction. Consider implementing one or two of the following examples:

- public acknowledgement of achievements
- recognition programs
- monthly or quarterly outings to promote staff bonding
- additional time off
- special parking space
- end of year trip upon reaching an annual financial goal
- monetary incentive plans

I particularly like Employee Incentive Plans as this is a wonderful motivator and, if crafted correctly, can be a key driver toward the practice's financial growth. A formal incentive plan allows staff to receive additional compensation by meeting certain revenue or conversion goals.

When creating a staff incentive plan, start with the business' financial goals in mind and develop the staff incentive around it (i.e. start with the end in mind). There are many incentive plan options to choose from, with the most popular being a reward over growth model. In this instance, staff members would receive a percentage of incoming revenue once an overall practice financial goal has been met.

Achieving the ultimate patient experience is highly dependent on your staff. If employees feel safe and taken care of, they will naturally take great care of your patients!

Step 3: Understanding the Patient Progression Lifecycle

"When you focus on the consumer, the consumer responds."
~ Alexander Wang

Once you have a winning team in place, it is time to fine-tune your practice processes. The absolute easiest way to do this is by breaking up the patient journey into "buckets" or stages, and then define key elements within each stage that can be used to propel the patient toward the path of making a buying decision. In marketing terms this is known as your "funnel."

As its name implies, your funnel is wider at the beginning and narrower at the end. You will have more patients starting a journey with your practice than completing the journey, as there will be buyers lost at each stage. This is a normal consumer occurrence as not everyone will be a fit for your practice, or even a candidate for their desired outcome. The key is to focus on those patients that ARE a match, build a strong relationship, and turn them into patient advocates.

A great metaphor (and very common in marketing) is to think of your funnel as a dating game. In the beginning stages you may be viewing dozens of profiles on a dating website, you may have friends offering to introduce you to what they claim to be the 'perfect match,' or maybe you are thinking a particular person in your building is cute.

If you're interested in initiating something further, you might reach out and say "Hello." Based on the success of this initial conversation, you may decide to meet for coffee or dinner. If you felt a connection you may decide to date exclusively, which could ultimately lead to marriage, then kids. You get the picture!

The point is, there is a potential point of exit during any of the stages in the dating game and understanding key drivers at each stage will help you to successfully navigate the funnel to achieve a desired outcome.

Your goal is to attract, engage and support patients at each stage in the process.
Your messaging at each stage will be different. What is appropriate at the "Marriage" stage most likely will not be appropriate at the "Hello" stage. Would you ask someone to marry you if you are still in the "hello" stage? Probably not.

Similar to the dating metaphor, patients will go through a progression funnel when interacting with your practice. You will need a consistent and strategic plan of communication at each stage that is in-line with where your patients are in terms of their relationship with you.

There are seven primary stages in the Patient Progression Lifecycle:

#1: Discover - This is essentially the point where a patient is made aware of your existence. You may be found through any number of platforms to include Google searches, word of mouth, social media, or paid advertising. In this stage the goal is to simply attract attention. You want to ensure your practice is meeting patients where they congregate.

Consider building your email list by offering access to a weekly blog. Begin posting relevant news and helpful information on Facebook. Share an interesting tweet that potential patients will appreciate on Twitter. Find a trusted review management company to help you get lots of ratings and reviews to gain social proof. Use your email lists to invite patients to live webinars hosted by a physician or staff member.

Facebook Live is very popular and is a great way to engage patients, both new and old. According to a Popular Science article, Facebook tweaked its algorithms in 2016 to show live video broadcasts higher up in people's news feeds. Nicola Mendelsohn, vice president for Facebook in Europe, Middle East, and Africa, said at the 2016 *Fortune's* Most Powerful Women International Summit that social network would "probably" be "all video" in the next half decade (Fortune Magazine, June 2016). So be a pioneer and start FB Live streams now!

Facebook Live topics are endless and could include "behind the scenes" segments, information on an exciting new injectable you are offering, a walk through the office's product area, a tour of the procedure or OR rooms (no patients of course – must comply with HIPAA regulations!).
Create a quick Facebook Live post showing a new shipment of skin care product that just arrived and offer one lucky viewer to receive a jar of the new "Magic Skin Cream" just by liking & replying to the post. Or even better – by sharing the post! Social sharing gets your practice in front of many new patient prospects very quickly.

These are just a few excellent ways to establish your practice as an industry leader, drive organic traffic to your practice, and engage your practice community.

#2: Initiate – In this stage a potential patient contacts the practice to either request information (such as cost) or to make an appointment. This is usually via phone call but could also happen at a meeting or via email. In the aforementioned dating analogy, this would be the "Hi, nice to meet you" stage.

This initial contact is an extremely important entry point as it has the ability to not only influence the patient's decision to make an appointment but is also statistically proven to help drive conversion rates at consultation.

Prepared patients are patients that buy. Unfortunately, many practices do not use this important contact as an opportunity to prepare the patient at all. This initial touchpoint should engage the patient and begin the practice/patient relationship. This is also the time to make sure the patient is, in fact, a candidate for the procedure they are requesting. This is not the time to simply schedule an appointment and hang up the phone.

Ideally, you can overcome most potential objections during this initial contact and would not have the need to address them at consult -- who wouldn't like that! A successful first call accomplishes the following:

- Builds the relationship through communication, connection, and empathy. Patients have a perceived problem they hope you can help them solve, and in order to help them, you must first develop a relationship. The relationship starts by simply providing your name. Ask the patient's name and use it often in the conversation. Provide other staff member names (when applicable). Present your practice as a team whose only mission in life is to be there for the patient. Engage the patient by listening to their needs but stay in control of the conversation by asking questions. Let the patient know exactly what to expect during their consultation or procedure so they will be well prepared.

- Ask qualifying questions to make sure the patient is actually a candidate for the procedure they are requesting. For instance, let's say a patient thinks they need liposuction of the abdomen, so they call the office and ask for the cost of liposuction. In reality, they may require a tummy tuck which could be 2-3 times the cost of the liposuction procedure. If we simply quote them a liposuction fee range and schedule an appointment, we are doing the patient, and the practice, a disservice. Chances are high they show for consultation, are told they require an abdominoplasty, have "sticker shock" when provided a quote estimate, and leave the practice without scheduling a procedure. In this example, you would ask questions to determine if the patient has excess skin or muscle laxity that would require a tummy tuck. For example, you might ask if they have sagging skin as a result of childbirth (as this is often a root cause of loose abdominal skin). You might also ask if they have stretch marks in their abdomen as this is indicative of little-to-no skin elasticity. If it appears the patient could be an abdominoplasty candidate upon asking qualifying questions, you should present the patient with an abdominoplasty estimate as well. Example would be, *"Based on the information you provided it sounds like you could be a tummy tuck candidate. We will not know for sure until you visit with Dr. Wonderful. In the interim, I am going to give you verbal estimates on both liposuction of the abdomen as well as a tummy tuck. Liposuction cost is..."* The key here is you want the patient to be prepared when they arrive at consultation with a realistic fee range. As well, this allows them to accurately prepare with financing companies if applicable.
- Overcome common objections prior to the consultation. Provide fee ranges if possible, even if the

21

patient does not ask! Starting the money conversation on the first call alleviates the dreaded money conversation at consult. Educate the caller on a procedure to include any potential deal breakers such as scarring, recovery limitations (i.e. they will not be able to pick up their 2 year old child for three weeks), and recovery time (they may not realize a procedure will require extra time off of work).

- Provide pertinent information on the provider of interest. For instance, does your doctor perform 200+ breast augmentations per year? You definitely want to let a breast augmentation prospect know this!

- Present a call to action. Using the either / or closing method, you might say, "Dr. Wonderful has an open consultation slot this Thursday at 11:00 am or Monday at 2:00 pm. Do either of these times work for you?"

- Confirm next steps. Let the patient know they will be able to schedule a procedure the day of their consultation. Ask if they require help obtaining financial assistance. Make sure there are no additional questions you can help them with at this time, and ensure they have your contact information should they have further questions prior to consultation. Let them know they will receive info via mail or email, and a confirmation call two days prior to their appointment.

#3: Action - At this stage the patient has decided to take action and make an appointment with your practice. The appointment could be for a Consultation or a Non-Surgical Procedure (laser procedure, fillers, facial, etc.). It is important to remember here that just because a patient or client makes an appointment, it does not mean they will show up! We must keep the patient engaged during this time, especially if you are unable to accommodate the patient's timeframe. Ideas for keeping the patient engaged:

- Send nicely appointed collateral for the patient to view to include information on their procedure of interest, information on the provider/practice/spa, or a "Welcome" or "Looking Forward to Meeting You" letter.
- Encourage the patient to visit your website to view Before & After photos, procedure information, and online videos.
- Invite the patient to read reviews and testimonials on your website or other platforms via email link. This provides social proof.
- Encourage the patient to follow you on Facebook or other social media platforms to keep up with the latest trends & news.
- Send relevant blogs you have written to the patient to further position yourself as a thought leader in the industry.
- Ensure the patient has your name and direct contact information should they have additional questions.

It is also imperative at this stage to conduct a reminder call to the patient prior to their appointment. Generally, this call should be made 2 days in advance of the appointment in order to allow the patient time to make arrangements with work, childcare, etc., in the event they had forgotten their appointment date or time. This call should be a continuation of the initial phone conversation, a method to continue the bonding process, and another chance to make sure the patient has no additional questions prior to their strategy session.

#4: **Strategy** – At this stage, the patient has physically shown up to the practice for a treatment strategy session with your office. This will be the first of a "series of firsts" the patient will have with your office.

Continuing with the dating analogy, consider this the "coffee or dinner" stage. If the conversation is good and you have confidence your "date" has the ability to meet your relationship goals and needs, then you will most likely continue the relationship with subsequent "dates" or commitments.

Along the same line, patients want to feel confident your practice will give them the results they are hoping to achieve. Hopefully by this point you have already built their confidence by positioning yourself as a thought leader in the industry, and by providing social proof through glowing testimonies, ratings & reviews. You have also started the bonding and education process on the first phone call, have vetted the patient by asking qualifying questions, and have prepared the patient for the consultation session. By the time the patient arrives to your office they should be so prepared that, at this point, they only require confirmation that 1) they like you, 2) you like them, and 3) you will be able to provide their desired outcome.

Think of the consultation as a "meet & greet" in addition to a strategic treatment planning session. If the patient does not feel a connection on this first "date," the likelihood they will move forward to the next stage is slim to none.

A successful strategy session will accomplish the following objectives:

- Continues the bonding process to incorporate all members of the team.
- Provides the patient with confidence that you are capable of delivering their desired result.

- Creates a treatment plan that will give the patient their best outcome.
- Arms the patient with pertinent information they will need to make the best decision.
- Educates the patient on all aspects of the procedure to include what to expect pre- and post-procedure
- Presents quote estimates (which should be in-line with patient expectations if it was discussed on the initial phone call!)
- Call to action (schedule the procedure) using the Either / Or closing method

#5: Commit - At this stage, the patient has scheduled a procedure or surgery with your office which is great! However, this does not mean the patient will complete surgery and, as mentioned in the Initiate Stage, they will need continued nurturing during this time.

It is at this stage the aesthetic patient begins demonstrating more "patient behaviors" than "consumer behaviors." This is when the reality kicks in.

Friends and family may question their judgement: "What if something happens to you? What will happen to your kids?"

Or the patient may see a magazine while waiting in line at the grocery store with the headline screaming: "Plastic Surgery Gone Bad!" and showing horrific images of famous movie stars with bad plastic surgery outcomes.

This is the time for the practice to be proactive. Adopt a "You've got this, and we've got you!!" approach. Remind the patient of the reason they came to see you in the first place, and how you are going to help them. Help them to stay focused on the end result. Be their cheerleader.

Ideas to nurture the relationship at this time include:

- Send a handwritten note thanking them for entrusting in you to be their surgeon and let them know they are in good hands.
- Schedule a "prep" call or office visit to ensure the patient will have everything they need, but may not realize they need, post-surgery (garments, meds, gauze, tape, cold packs, nursing service, transportation, childcare, animal care, pre-prepared meals, special clothing, etc.).
- Provide the patient with a Pre- & Post-Procedure Checklist.
- Invite caretakers to participate in the pre-op visit and have a special checklist and "What to expect" letter for them.
- Consider a post-procedure gift bag with a few items the patient will need in the days or weeks following their procedure. This could include gauze, tape, cold packs, a can of Chicken Noodle Soup, or even a practice branded and comfortable t-shirt.
- Call the patient the night before their procedure. Let them know you will be going to bed early that evening and will be looking forward to seeing them in the morning.

#6: Implement - During this stage the patient shows up for, and proceeds with, the chosen procedure. After the procedure, the immediate focus is usually on pain management and the comfort of the patient, as it should be. Making sure the patient has access to the practice at all times is essential.

If anything, the Implement Stage is when a patient is most vulnerable. They are questioning their decision to have a procedure. They are probably in pain. And, as you know, are probably seeing things look a bit "wonky" as the healing process begins. Things that are very normal to a practice may seem incredibly wrong to a patient. This could include asymmetrical swelling or unexpected pain. It is during this time patients need your reassurance, presence, and nurturing the most.

Ways to continue the relationship building with the patient during this stage include the following:

- Post-surgical calls to the patient by the surgeon, nurse, and even the patient coordinator (on different times/days) show the patient you are there for them, and that just because they have completed surgery does not mean they have been forgotten.
- If possible, have an alternative entryway, or back door, patients can use for their post-surgical visits. This is beneficial not only to the patient (as they can be brought directly to an exam room and made comfortable very quickly), but also to the practice (so potential patients in the reception area are not seeing the recovery phase of a procedure, potentially causing them to question their decision to have surgery).
- Consider a post-surgical gift or card. This does not have to be expensive and can be something as simple as a bouquet of flowers. Many florists will partner with a practice to provide discounted pricing as long as they know you will be buying from them on a consistent basis. Gift cards that relate to the procedure are also a great idea. For instance, you may consider a Victoria's Secret gift card for a patient who just had a breast augmentation.

#7: Tribe / Community – The biggest cost to any business is the cost to acquire a new customer. So, once a patient becomes a customer, what are you doing to make sure you are providing ongoing and relevant content to continue the connection?

As previously mentioned, satisfied patients will go elsewhere if they are presented with a better perceived "deal." The goal is to move your patients beyond the satisfied stage and into an Emotionally Invested stage.

By understanding and proactively addressing a patient's needs at each stage as listed here in this book, you have undoubtedly built a strong and lasting relationship with your patients. Continue to enhance the relationship by providing invaluable resources, a sense of community, and special perks:

- Stay in front of your patients through social media and email. Provide them with information on new procedures and products they may be interested in, or on the latest and greatest aesthetic trends.
- Host "Patient Appreciation" or "VIP" events. This could be a drop-in ice cream social, a new product release preview party, or any event that provides the patient with a feeling of exclusivity.
- Send a handwritten note with a gift certificate that is NOT associated with your practice when a patient refers a buying customer. A great example is a $5 "Thanks a Latte!" gift card from Starbucks.
- Start a Membership program that provides patients with exclusive discounts and other VIP benefits.
- Send a monthly newsletter with specials, new products, articles, and even news on what's happening in the practice (i.e. "Dr. Wonderful just returned from a mission

trip to Haiti" or "Nurse Amanda welcomes a healthy baby boy!").

In closing, the patient will move through a series of stages before becoming a patient advocate. It is imperative to have systems in place at each one of these stages to help the patient move easily to the next stage and reduce client loss. You must nurture the relationship through ongoing communication. With the proper systems in place, it is simply a 'no-brainer' for the patient to advance through each subsequent stage.

Step 4: DO Sweat The Small Things

"A man's accomplishments in life are the cumulative effect of his attention to detail."
~ John Foster Dulles

A patient's relationship with your practice consists of a series of "firsts." This will include the first time they became aware of your practice, the first time they speak with you on the phone, the first time they arrive and are greeted in your practice, the first time they meet each team member, and possibly the first time they have ever had a procedure at all.

That said, everything that happens after the "firsts" are also detrimental. Consider this: my rescued Thoroughbred required veterinary care several years ago, so I contacted a local and reputable vet to come and attend to her. He showed knowledge and took great care of her. I just loved him! Unfortunately, most subsequent contacts were not so great.

Sadly, it was not the doctor but a staff member that ruined our patient / veterinarian relationship. To say his receptionist was unpleasant is putting it mildly. She was non-committal or bored at best, and downright rude at worst. It was difficult to schedule appointments as their scheduling system was always down. I eventually ended up transferring to another veterinarian.

Unfortunately, this doctor never knew the reason he lost a client as I'm sure he was never made aware of the difficult interactions I had with his employee. Now more than ever patients are taking to review sites and social media to leave ratings and reviews, which means every interaction you have with your patient counts.

Make every contact stand out by paying attention to the smallest of details. There are 5 traditionally recognized senses: sight, sound, touch, taste, and smell. Successful practices understand the need to engage all five senses when considering the patient experience. To follow are suggestions to engage each of the patient's senses and help create a favorable experience with your practice:

Sight
- The exterior of the building is just as important as the interior of your practice. It should be welcoming, clean, and easy to access.
- The reception area should be inviting and welcoming as soon as the patient enters. Whether the décor has a residential feel (think plants, throw rugs, lamps, and comfortable furniture) or a more modern and sleek approach, the patient should be visually captivated.
- Magazines and other reading material should be up-to-date and relevant to your target audience (i.e. if you see mostly females you probably do not need 12 issues of a hunting magazine as part of your reading arsenal).
- Add a Testimonials book to a table in the reception area so patients can read the wonderful feedback your practice has received and get them in a 'buying' frame of mind.
- Attention to cleanliness is paramount in all areas of the practice. Staff members should circulate the premises often throughout the day to make sure there is no trash lying about.
- If the practice has no natural light or windows, consider white (not colored!) plant lights for plants and/or soft

lighting from lamps. Avoid harsh fluorescent lights if possible.

- Attention to detail in the exam room will elevate the patient's perception of the practice. Elegant mirrors add a special touch as they will be a focal point to "frame" the patient when discussing potential procedure options. Cloth hangers or wicker baskets that can be used for the patient's clothing are nice touches. I've also seen practices use luxury sheets on the exam table in the consultation room instead of paper to elevate the patient experience.
- All patient registration forms and other collateral can be presented in leather menus for an elevated touch.
- Consider nicely branded folders for patients to take home. The folders should include information on the procedure of interest, quote estimate(s), and other pertinent information.

Sound
- Music should reflect the preference of your patient base. For instance, Facial Plastic Surgeons generally have an older patient base and should approach music targeted to this demographic. Face & body practices, on the other hand, tend to have a wider age gap, so neutral or relaxing music throughout the office would be best here. This does not have to be an expensive overhead stereo system. It could be something as simple as a Bluetooth speaker in each room playing music from a designated source.
- Attention to staff conversations. The patient is always listening and does not need to overhear a conversation about the fight you just had with your significant other, or the difficult patient that was seen earlier in the day.
- Attention to practice-patient conversations. Can other patients hear your conversations through the exam room

walls? If yes, consider a noise machine, music, or in-room TV monitor to drown out private conversations.

- Water features are proven to be relaxing and inviting and can also be used as a noise blocker. Consider small individual features throughout the office.

Touch

- Room temperature – is your office too warm? Too cool? While we may on our feet and running around the office all day, we must remember the patient is generally idle during the exam or treatment and is oftentimes without clothing.
- Robes and blankets should be soft to the touch, unless the patient is being seen for a post-operative procedure in which paper robes are required. Consider investing in a blanket warmer and provide patients with a toasty robe to wear during the consultation & exam during winter seasons.
- Ensure all items the patient will touch are cleaned throughout the day. This includes door handles, beverage stations, and even pens & clipboards.

Taste

- Beverage station to include coffee, flavored water, or tea.
- Small bottled waters distributed by staff.
- Individually wrapped candies, mints, or cookies.

Smell

- Should be pleasant but not overwhelming.
- Robes and blankets should not smell like perfume from a previous patient (trust me, this seems like common sense, but I've witnessed these more times than I care to remember).

- No offensive smelling food allowed in the break room! This means no fish, Brussel sprouts, or burnt popcorn.
- Candles are always a nice touch, especially when used in the restrooms.

Take the patient on a journey of their senses with your practice to enhance the overall experience. Tap into that emotion we discussed earlier. Help them imagine life on the other side of their procedure.

Step 5: Sales

"Pretend that every single person you meet has a sign around his or her neck that says, 'Make me feel important.' Not only will you succeed in sales, you will succeed in life."
~ Mary Kay Ash

Sales really gets a bad rap. No one likes a pushy salesperson, and no one wants to be a pushy salesperson. That said, sales are an instrumental part of our everyday existence. Without sales we would have no economy. Think about that!

According to a study by Bain & Company, a whopping 81% of consumers buy between the 5th and 12th touchpoint. Adversely, 90% of salespeople stop following up before the 5th touchpoint with the consumer (source: American Marketing Association).

This is huge! Think about it – if you are one of the 10% that keeps in touch with potential patients you are way ahead in the game, and chances are the patient will choose your practice when they are ready to buy.

Many years ago, I learned the phrase "retail medicine." The concept of retail medicine is that the aesthetic patient demonstrates more consumer (or 'shopping') behaviors than actual patient behaviors. Their healthcare provider is not dictated by an insurance company. Instead, cosmetic patients are free to choose their preferred provider.

This consumerism "upped the ante" for aesthetic providers everywhere, and a new mindset on internal marketing and sales processes had to be adopted. The consumer patient demands the same elevated experience from their cosmetic providers as they expect from any other service-oriented place of business (restaurants, hotels, etc.). If the experience does not match or exceed their expectations, they will simply find another business that does.

Once the concept of retail medicine and its role in the aesthetic practice is that specialized sales processes must be embraced by all. Sales does not have to be pushy or manipulative. When approached correctly, a well-defined sales process actually helps the patient make the best decisions, while also relaying the message that they will be taken great care of in the process. By making a few changes to mindset, sales can actually be the easiest part of the patient relationship!
Think of the sales process as a conversation you are having with your patient. This is where you are able to find out what's important to patients and what their objections are. By understanding the patient's needs, and by building a relationship with the patient in the beginning stages, choosing to move forward with your practice should just be the next logical step in the process.

A successful sales process is one that is strategic, documented, repeatable, and measurable. There should be prescribed actions in place for every stage of the Patient Progression Lifecycle. Again, consistency is key. You should not be re-inventing the wheel for each patient, nor should you be randomly taking actions that do not serve you or the patient in your sales process.

Sales processes should be very detailed and will include the exact steps a practice will take to move the patient toward the outcome they wish to achieve. For example, in the Initiation stage, if the patient did not schedule an appointment, you may implement the following actions:

1. Send procedure and practice information to the patient the day of Initiation.
2. Follow-up phone call 2 days post patient initiation to ensure the patient does not have additional questions, and to see if they are ready to schedule an appointment.
3. Send a Testimonials letter to the patient via email and or snail mail 7 days post initiation call.
4. Follow-up phone call 10 days post patient initiation to confirm they received the information you sent and encourage them to view your website to see before & after photos.

Each of these touchpoints should have a call to action. Each contact should also let the patient know the next steps. This could be a statement as simple as, "It is great catching up with you today. I am going to send over some patient testimonials and additional procedure information. I will call you in a couple of days to make sure you received them!"

When the patient says "Ok" or agrees to your follow-up, they are providing you with permission to follow-up, and believe it or not they will be expecting that follow-up. Think about the many times you call a patient and they say, "I have been meaning to call you!"

There could be any number of touchpoints at any stage. I have seen practices have great success with only 3-4 contacts at each stage and others that require many more contacts with the patient. This is why it is imperative to measure conversion rates to see what is working and what is not working. Throw out actions that do not work and keep those that do.

Most practice management systems on the market today have automated sales function capability. You will hear them called Action Items, Action Groups, Ladders, Tasks, etc. Regardless of the name, you are essentially setting up strategies to help the patient move easily through the stages in your funnel. This is your sales process – your business plan for success!

If your practice management system does not have automated funnel reminders, simply create a document listing each of the stages in the Patient Progression Lifecycle and outline what follow-up steps you will take at each stage.

Either way, the touchpoints should include phone call follow up as well as written follow-up. The touchpoints should be precise (i.e. exactly what letter is to be sent?) and list the exact day it should be completed.

All correspondence should be pre-prepared so that it is consistent with your brand and core messaging. That said, I do recommend leaving room in a form letter for a personal sentence or two acknowledging the patient's specific concerns. This adds a personal touch to the letter and further assures the patient you were listening to them during the conversation.

I recently heard an analogy that selling and sales are a lot like the game of golf. Both require skill, a lot of practice, and technique. Setting up your touchpoint business plan is the "technique" in this formula. "Practice" is in the repetition.

Skill, however, is learned. And one of the best skills you can master in the sales environment is the art of overcoming objections. In the game of golf, you have what is known as the long ball and the short ball. The long shots travel great distances in order to position the ball as close to the hole as possible. The long ball essentially sets the stage for the short ball (a chip or putt) to make the hole.

In sales, the long ball is everything leading up to the consultation. It is all of the touchpoints in the Discover, Initiate, Action, and Commit stages (to include online presence and social proof, marketing endeavors, and all of the aforementioned "firsts" included in the Strategy stage).

If done correctly, the long ball addresses all potential objections a patient may have so that by the time a patient reaches the Strategy stage, or Consultation, it is simply a matter of hitting the short ball and closing the deal.

In other words, if you make your touchpoints work for you, there should be no objections to overcome. The long ball should be so powerful that you should almost be able to hit a hole in one with no selling actually required at consultation!

Common objections include cost, financing, scarring, time off from work, recovery, provider availability, patient desired timeframe, or unsupportive family members. Cover these during initial contacts with your patients and ideally you will not find the need to overcome them at consultation.

Once you have overcome any objections the patient may have, you will need to provide a call to action. This could be a simple question such as, "Dr. Wonderful is available Tuesday October 24th at 7am if that works for you? You will be his first case on that day which I know most patients prefer!" If the patient is not ready to commit let them know you understand and have a follow-up plan in place (i.e. your touchpoints business plan).

Simply put, the sales process is essentially building a relationship with the patient, employing strategic actions repeatedly and consistently, overcoming common objections, and putting forth a call to action. You've got this!

Step 6: Measure To Manage

"If you can't manage it, you can't improve it." ~ Peter Drucker

This is, undoubtedly, one of the most important quotes in business management. How do you know if you are succeeding if you do not measure? If you do not have benchmarking data, how can you grow your practice?

While data at any level is significant, there are certain measurements every practice should know and pull on a monthly, quarterly, bi-annual, and annual basis:

Conversion data: How do you know how well your practice is moving your patients through the Patient Progression Lifecycle? It may 'feel' like you convert 50% of your consultation patients to surgery, but is this actually the case? Most practice management software systems on the market today have the capability to run conversion reports for each stage of the patient journey. Use the data to identify areas of opportunity for growth and implement actions to improve. If the conversion rates go up, you know you are on the right track!

Procedure data: What are your highest performing procedures in terms of count, revenue, and revenue per hour? This is important as you want to focus on procedures that drive revenue to the practice. Sometimes you may find the procedure you consider to be a 'cash cow' is in fact hindering financial growth.

Provider data: Know the difference between provider and staff performance in your practice. For instance, a practice's overall No Show / Appointment Cancellation Rate might be 30%, which is very high. However, staff member "A" actually has an acceptable rate of 15%, while staff member "B" has an extremely poor rate of 45%. By measuring their performance, you can quickly determine staff member "B" needs additional phone skills training and/or needs to be removed from the appointment making process altogether.

Discounting data: Is 'over discounting' contributing to stalled revenue? Do you know the average discount your practice is offering across all procedures?

Source data: This data is crucial if you are spending money on advertising. What is your return on your advertising investment? Are you throwing money out the window? Or maybe there is a particular patient advocate that has sent you many patients; you definitely want to thank them! Most practices gather source data only when the patient shows for consultation, and some not until a procedure has been completed. I recommend obtaining this at the first point of contact – even if an appointment is not made. You see, just like with patients, referral sources have scheduling rates and cancellation rates. By knowing that last month's magazine ad generated 50 inquiries but only 4 appointments, you are able to see the opportunity is there and perhaps you need to refine your phone message to capture this segment of patients.

Patient surveys: While practice management software can often tell you <u>where</u> there is a patient/practice disconnect, it cannot tell you <u>why</u> the disconnect is present.
This leaves it up to the practice to try and figure out the issues. By using patient surveys, you are able to understand the reasons "straight from the patient's mouth."
For instance, say a large percentage of patients report being confused by the quote estimate during consultation. This

coupled with a lower than average consultation to surgery conversion rate defines an area of opportunity for practice growth. You may need to update the physical quote to include more concise and easier to understand language. You may need to conduct further education for your Patient Coordinator on their delivery message.

The point is, the low consult – scheduled conversion rate report lets you know something was amiss at consultation, but the patient feedback from the survey let you know why.

Telephone Secret Shopper calls: Okay, I agree secret shopper calls are not actually what comes to mind when thinking of data and analytics, but they should be an important part of your information gathering arsenal. How is your staff engaging your new patient callers? Are they asking questions and providing information – even if not asked? Are they promoting their provider and procedures? Are they qualifying the patient? What makes this call different than all of the other calls we know the consumer patient is making as they "shop" for a provider? Secret shopper calls are helpful to identify areas of opportunity to include phone skills training and consistency.

Year-Over-Year data: A year-over-year is a comparison of a statistic for one period to the same period in the previous year. This is usually monthly or quarterly and calculates the percentage change in growth (or decline) during the time period. A YOY report is helpful because it removes any effects of seasonality and also identifies long term trends.

In summary, monitoring practice performance data is key in order to providing an ultimate patient experience with your practice. Patients are letting the practice know their thoughts and perceptions with each action they make. Luckily, we can use data to write their story, and then use their story to make adjustments that will enhance the patient journey. This increases retention and referral and helps maximize profitability.

Step 7: Product

"Great companies are built on great products." ~ Elan Musk

In the aesthetics realm, your main "Product" is the procedural outcome, right? Well, not so fast... It turns out the overall experience a patient has with your practice may trump an excellent surgical or procedural outcome.

Could this be why there are so many great surgeons that are barely able to stay in business, and a ton of "not so great surgeons" with a surplus of patients knocking down their doors?

The differentiating factor is the overall patient experience. It is an accumulation of every single touchpoint the patient experiences with a practice, and the relationship built along the way. Even if the outcome of a procedure is not perfect, a patient is still likely to recommend the practice to their friends if they feel they connected and had rapport with the doctor and staff.

Dr. Wendy Levinson with the University of Toronto is considered to be one of the foremost researchers on physician-patient communication. In a landmark 1997 study (as reported in the February 19, 1997 JAMA Journal), she recorded hundreds of conversations between a group of physicians and their patients. Half of the doctors had never been sued, and the other half had been sued at least twice. On the basis of those recorded conversations alone, she found significant differences in patient interactions between the two groups:

- The doctors who had never been sued spent more than three minutes longer with each patient than those who had been sued (18.3 minutes versus 15 minutes).

- The doctors who had never been sued were more likely to make "orienting" comments, such as "First I'll examine you, and then we will talk the problem over" or "I will leave time for your questions."
- The doctors who had never been sued were more likely to engage in active listening, saying things such as "Go on, tell me more about that."
- They were far more likely to laugh and be funny during the visit.

Dr. Levinson found there was actually no difference in the amount or quality of information physicians gave their patients. She discovered the never-sued doctors did not provide any more details about medication or the patient's condition. The difference was entirely in how they talked to and communicated with their patients.

There have been many similar studies that support Dr. Levinson's findings. What does this mean to you, and why am I bringing this up in the Procedure chapter of the book?

A successful procedural outcome is of utmost importance but may not be the only driver of patient satisfaction and advocacy. Combining a wonderful procedural outcome with clear communication and relationship building via strategic processes will lead to the Ultimate Patient Experience every time!

Final Thoughts

I hope you enjoyed reading this book and were able to gleam at least a few pearls of wisdom you can start using immediately within your practice. As mentioned throughout the manuscript, implementation and consistency will be key to achieving successful outcomes.

I always welcome comments and thoughts! Feel free to email me anytime at info@ashley-cloud.com.

I also encourage you to visit www.ashley-cloud.com for information on Practice Management Consulting, Staff Development, and other services we provide.

To request a **complimentary telephone secret shopper** call to your practice click here, or visit https://calendly.com/ashley-cloud to access a scheduler.

I look forward to connecting soon!

Ashley

NOTES:

NOTES:

NOTES:

NOTES:

NOTES: -

NOTES:

NOTES:

NOTES:

NOTES:

NOTES:

Printed in Great Britain
by Amazon

38339830R00040